Klee

Text *by*
ROBERT FISHER

Edited *by*
THEODORE REFF
Associate Professor of Art History
Columbia University

TUDOR PUBLISHING COMPANY
New York

Published by

TUDOR PUBLISHING COMPANY

New York, 1967

Library of Congress Catalog Card Number: 66-10559

All reproduction rights reserved by S.P.A.D.E.M., Paris

Printed in Japan

KLEE, THE POET-PAINTER

Attempting to unite on canvas the disparate disciplines of painting, poetry, music and architecture, the Swiss painter Paul Klee consumed himself with a passion for communicating the incomprehensible. He sought to take the viewer beyond the concepts of language, beyond the idea that the real world is what we see, and to remind those who looked at his works that life is full of mysteries. The real for him was the universe of self-expression through art, and the signs and symbols he painted were adumbrations of what he felt to be the true but hidden nature of the world. His mission, he preached constantly, was to make visible that which is invisible to most of us.

Preoccupation with "reality"

From his lectures on art and from his essays on the discipline of painting, we know a great deal of what he was trying to say. Nevertheless, as he did not explicity comment on each canvas as it was created, we can only speculate about the meaning of most of his works. We know what were his stated attitudes toward space, symbolism and form, but we also know that his paintings resulted from the same kind of subjective forces as exist for all artists in all times. This was particularly true toward the end of his life, when he became obsessed with death and attempted to portray the face of this final mystery and his feelings toward it. As human as the world allowed him to be, he feared death and yet, in his remarkable last series of paintings, seemed to come to terms with it in perhaps as significant a way as is possible in art.

The mysteries of life

In the last two years of his life, he produced 1,500 of

3

the total 9,000 works completed in his 42 years of creative activity. Before he died, in 1940, he had reached the ultimate, for his time and for his character, in expressing the unknown world for those of us who believe only in the world as we ordinarily see and understand it.

Born in Switzerland on December 18, 1879, Klee was to live nearly thirty years in Germany, where he learned to paint and where he spent his adult life prior to becoming chronically ill. In the town of Münchenbuchsee, near Bern, where he was born of a German music teacher and a Swiss mother, he remained only one year. In 1880, his family moved to Bern, where he spent a quiet childhood, steeped in the traditions of a pedagogic background. His mother was a gentle woman, his father a stern but indulgent teacher of the old school. Until nineteen, Klee seemed like any other young lad of intellectual bent, as he attended primary school and then the high school. He learned to play the violin at the age of seven, and practiced daily, pleasing his parents but annoying neighbors.

Early years— Bern

He had long since decided he wished to be an artist, and in 1898, with his family's blessing, went to Munich, where he enrolled in the Knirr School of Art. He had previously wavered for some time, nevertheless, unable to make up his mind whether to be a musician, a poet, or a painter, and when he made the decision, he did not altogether abandon the other fields. Throughout his life he attempted to portray music in paint and to combine poetry and color on canvas.

Munich and art training

Munich in 1898 was a hotbed of artistic endeavor with anxious young Germans eager to expand the Romantic school to its natural, Germanic, peak (or so they thought) and a few, like Hans Arp, Franz Marc and Kandinsky hopeful of creating new forms in art. In October, 1900, Klee was accepted by Franz Stuck as an apprentice in his studio and at the same time entered Stuck's class at the Munich Academy, where he spent a year. During these three years in Munich, Paul studied the usual courses, including anatomy, etching and art history. In 1899, he also met the pianist Lily Stumpf, who inspired him and eventually became his wife, in 1906.

Fired with enthusiasm for the profession of painting, but still uncertain of his direction or ability, he determined to take a long trip to Italy, the traditional land of inspiration for the artist. With Hermann Haller, he set out in 1901 for a journey which would take six months. He was entranced by the colors of the sun-drenched Mediterranean, but tended to be more interested in the new Italy rather than the old, experiencing one of the greatest joys of the trip in the magnificently-equipped aquarium in Naples. Unusual at the time were the glass display cases in which he could see an amazing variety of colorful fish living in an artificial world which to them was "reality." The impression lasted and influenced his later declarations of artistic philosophy.

Italy

Returning from Italy, Klee decided to live in Bern, where he stayed for three years, etching a little and serving in the Bern Symphony Orchestra as a violinist. He was beginning to formulate his own concept of painting, and wrote in his diary: "I can hardly bear the thought of having to live in a period of mere imitation in art.... There are three things at the present time: Greco-Roman antiquity (*physis*), with an objective outlook, worldly aims and emphasis on structure, and Christianity (*psyche*), with a subjective outlook, otherworldly aim and emphasis on music. The third consists in being modest, ignorant and self-taught, a 'tiny Ego.' I'm learning from scratch, I'm beginning to create as if I know nothing at all about painting." His declaration of independence from all he had learned at

Bern—
first
steps to
art
theory

5

the schools in Munich was definite and uncomplicated—he meant to begin all over again, and by himself, on his own terms, to study art.

He began to paint and to produce a series of excellent etchings which demonstrated his mastery of draughtsmanship. In 1905, eager to expand his horizons, he visited Paris, but only briefly, and apparently made no contact whatsoever with the Fauves or their work. In the two weeks he spent there, with his friends Bloesch and Moilliet, he visited the museums and the cabarets, but seemed to be scarcely influenced by what he saw. To be sure, he admired the works of Velàsquez, Goya and Manet, about whom he had already studied; but in his diary he wrote that he had nothing to learn from the French. He seems to have been unaware that the struggle he was going through to find a new meaning in art was the same which the young French artists were themselves experiencing.

Paris

Marriage and return to Munich

In September, 1906, Klee married Lily Stumpf and took her to Munich, where they settled down, "alone in the midst of 5,000 artists," as he put it in his diary. When a child was born, he had to stay home and take care of it while his wife went out teaching piano lessons. He was commissioned to do some portraits, but for a few years received nothing but rejection from the powers of the artistic community. His works were returned by publications and exhibition committees, he was refused membership in an artists' association, and half his paintings were rejected by the Munich Sezession (exhibition). However, he was employed for a few months in 1908 by an art school, and, of course, having half his submitted works (three) accepted by the Sezession was better than having none accepted.

The next few years were spent in quiet preparation for his life work, although he was constantly disturbed by not being able to put his finger on the source of his lack of

inspiration. He dealt mainly in linear work, etchings, constructions and *tours-de-force* of marvelous interlocking lines
and objects. But nothing seemed to spell fire and success.
By 1910, intrigued by the works of Van Gogh and intensely
stirred by Cézanne, he had begun to experiment with his
own techniques and to reconsider his approach to art. In
that year, he exhibited more than fifty of his drawings,
paintings and sketches at the Bern Museum, and also had
shows in Zürich and Winterthur.

*Linear
experi-
ments*

The next year, after two years of work, Klee finished his
illustrations to *Candide,* which he hoped to sell to a
Munich publisher. He failed to do so, however, and sought
consolation in the company of other artists, helping to found
a group known as Sema. Through his increased interest in
the work of other painters, he met Kandinsky, Franz Marc
and Hans Arp, all in 1911. Intrigued with the Blaue Reiter
(Blue Rider) group, Klee joined them in their second exhibition in 1912. The aim of the group, according to
Kandinsky, was "to show, in the variety of styles re-
presented, how the artist's innermost desires can take form
in every conceivable manner." Klee felt that the principles
advocated by the Blaue Reiter provided him with the perfect
tools to express his inner musical and poetic emotions.

*The
Blaue
Reiter*

In 1912, Klee again visited Paris, meeting Robert
Delaunay, who was to have a great influence on him.
There, in Delaunay's studios, Klee was introduced to
Cubism. During his trip he also saw the works of Rousseau,
Braque and Picasso, as well as Cubist paintings by Vlaminck
and Derain. And though he derided Cubism, he cor-
responded with Delaunay, absorbing the latter's opinions on
light and color, and realizing that he was perhaps not alone
in his search for a new meaning for the craft of painting.

*Paris—
Delaunay
and
Cubism*

Klee's awakening to his vocation did not actually come
until 1914, when he made his memorable trip to North

Africa. In spite of his education in the schools of art, it was not until he reached Tunis and saw the sun-spattered sands and turrets of the Arabs that he could say, "I am a painter." Nearly overwhelmed by his infatuation with the land, and even questioning his being—"Is this my native land?"—he finally grasped the significance of color. "I am entranced by color—I do not need to pursue it. I know that it will possess me until I die. This is the great moment— I and color are one. I am a painter."

Klee's diary in Tunis is filled with happy images, and in a few days' time, he came to realize how deep the strains of poetry were embedded in his existence. He became supremely aware of the importance of color to his chosen

field. His infatuation with certain images is also under-scored in his diary: "More than one blond rising moon of the north will call to me sweetly, like a blurred vision in a mirror. It will be my betrothed, my other self. But I, myself, am the moon rising in the south." Moons, the sands of Tunisia, the greens of its oases, the little cubes of Arab buildings with their triangular flags all occur over and over again in Klee's works from now until his death twenty-six years later. The patterns he saw on Arabian carpets, the mystic symbols on the leatherwork and textiles of the area combined with the colors and intriguing emotions of his visit to provide him with a dictionary of material from which he could draw for decades.

World War One broke out in August of the same year, and within eighteen months, Klee's friend Franz Marc was killed at the front and Klee himself was conscripted into the German army. He could have escaped this fate by returning to his Swiss homeland, but chose to remain in Munich with his friends, the artists and his adopted people. The war years were not a total loss for him. Although he felt stunted and oppressed by the atmosphere of fear, then

8

frenzy and finally despair, he was able to continue with his work even while he clerked in an army depot or painted airplane wings. In 1917, in fact, the Sturm Gallery in Berlin sold several of his works and he began to receive some public attention in the press and literary journals. It was during this period that he came to certain important conclusions. He wrote: "The more fearful this world becomes, the more abstract its art," and thought that perhaps only a happy world could produce realistic painting. The world created by war was too horrible to be *real;* it could only be a transition period, a temporary phase of existence, a delusion. "True reality lies invisible underneath all this." This preoccupation with the real and the unreal was to be a source of his energy and a major factor in his outpouring of fantastic, otherworldly paintings for the rest of his years.

*Philoso-
phy of
the real*

In the chaos that was post-war Germany, Klee applied for a teaching job at the Stuttgart Academy, but was rejected. Inspired, however, by his new grasp of color and the peace which the end of the war afforded him, he began to paint enthusiastically, selling several canvases and working on an essay on art. By 1920, he was ready to exhibit nearly 400 works in Munich. His sketches for *Candide* were finally published, and his work for another book, *Potsdamer Platz,* was also greeted by the public when that book was brought out. Most important, however, was the publication in 1920 of his essay, "Creative Confessions," in the Berlin review, *Tribüne der Kunst und Zeit.*

*"Creative
Confes-
sions"*

"Art does not reproduce the visible—it makes visible." With these words, Klee summed up his entire experience as an artist and laid the foundations for his work of the years to come. He continued, "A picture is constructed, piece by piece, like a building. The work of art is above all a process of creation—it is never merely a product."

He defined the formal elements of drawing as points, surface, space and the energy of the line being drawn. Movement, he said, is the essence of art. Everything moves, the painting itself and the eyelids and eyes of the viewer.

The Bauhaus

Amid the confusion of the building of a new Germany, the eminent architect Walter Gropius founded the Bauhaus in Weimar, an attempt to unite all the arts and put an end to the anarchy and frequent warfare between architecture, painting, sculpture, photography and other disciplines. One of the first men to be invited to join the faculty was Paul Klee. Feininger and Kandinsky were also to join. The differences between fine and applied arts were to be de-emphasized; craftsman and painter were to combine their approaches in the achievement of beauty.

Klee was extremely happy in the Bauhaus atmosphere. He worked with his dear friend Kandinsky at the school, and by night they and their wives met to have dinner, play music and occasionally attend the opera or ballet. Klee was not a particularly good teacher, but he enjoyed being constantly with fellow artists, and the period was a most fruitful one in his life. Exhibits continued, in Berlin, Wiesbaden, and, in 1924, even in New York. He published several works, lectured occasionally, and enjoyed watching his son approach adolescence.

The Blauen Vier

In 1924, Klee founded the Blauen Vier group in Weimar, together with Kandinsky, Feininger and Jawlensky. They hoped to have their own exhibitions and to reinforce their joint views on art by common action and teaching. In the same year, Klee briefly visited Sicily, renewing his acquaintance with the sun in a southern climate. The next year, the Bauhaus was forced out of Weimar by reactionaries opposed to the "dangerous experiments" going on there, and relocated in Dessau. Klee joined the first exhibition of Surrealist painters in Paris, as if to show his defiance to the Weimar opponents of modern trends. He also exhibited again in Munich. But the highlight of the year was his first one-man show in Paris, which was comparatively successful.

In 1924, at Jena, Klee lectured on modern art, laying down a few more principles, or refining them, further illustrating his increasingly consistent devotion to color: "Three main elements are...the line, which is purely dimensional ...tone value, which gives weight to a picture...and color, which gives the picture quality." Color is not only quality and weight, he said, but also dimension. He explained how a construction could become a composition and thus move from the realm of the abstract to art. This lecture, although not published until 1945, has had a continuing influence on artists ever since it was first delivered.

The Jena lecture

In 1926–27 and again in 1928, Klee made trips outside Germany. He visited Italy once and France twice, hoping, perhaps, to find new inspiration in new sights. Later, in 1928, he received a grant from a Brunswick art collector to visit Egypt, which he had often expressed a desire to see. Unlike his experiences in Tunisia, however, his reactions to Egypt were somewhat disappointing. He was not pleased with the tourists' Egypt and seemed to gain from the trip only a modest renewal of the forces and emotions which had already awakened in him in Tunis in 1914. Perhaps, sadly enough, age made the difference—when he had visited Tunisia and had been captivated by color, he was only 35; in Egypt he was already 49, a professor, lecturer and established celebrity of sorts. Perhaps, too, after the impact of Tunisia, Egypt may not have been unique enough for him. Upon his return to Germany in early 1929, he seemed restless, and made a trip to southern France and Spain. Exhibitions in Berlin and Paris, organized in

Egypt

celebration of his fiftieth birthday, helped somewhat to restore his spirits.

In 1931, in a pique over a minor matter at the Bauhaus, Klee resigned from that institution, moving to Düsseldorf, where he took a post at the academy. He made another trip to Sicily, visited Switzerland and Venice again, and seemed to be on the road to a continuing career of prosperity and increasing fame. In 1932, however, with the advent of the Nazis in Germany, his friend Kandinsky was hounded into returning to Russia, and Klee himself, though not a Jew, fell under attack by the Nazis and their supporters for his "decadent art." In 1933, on his return to Germany from a short trip to France, he found himself the object of severe controversy at the Düsseldorf Academy, where the local reactionaries were trying to have him fired. When the officials gave in to the pressure and dismissed him, Klee finally decided to move to Switzerland. Around Christmas of 1933, he left Germany forever, returning to Bern, where his sister was still living, and settled there.

Return to Switzerland

Klee's remaining years in Bern were peaceful, but beset by a number of difficulties which interfered with the contentment he hoped to find in his native country. Although born in Switzerland, he was technically a German, because of his father's nationality and his long sojourn in Germany. He applied for Swiss citizenship a few months before his death, but due to the usual red tape of modern bureaucracy it was not until a few weeks after he had died that Paul Klee was officially acknowledged as a son by his native land.

Increasing illness

In 1935, he began to suffer from the skin disease which eventually caused his death. His work, nevertheless, continued to develop. Exhibits in London, New York and Paris took place, followed in 1940 by a large exhibition of his paintings in Bern. As he experimented with colors and chalk, pen and brush, he also sensed the impending visit from the angel of Death. Having portrayed the "unreal" world all his life, however, confident that it was reality itself, he now felt little fear when face to face with the knowledge of his own departure from what others regarded as reality.

His last work, *Still Life* (Plate 91), depicts Jacob and the angel wrestling, yet strangely uniting and becoming one. *Jacob and the angel* Perhaps feeling that angels are the pilots between the two worlds, both real, which all men must experience, Klee left behind a message in this last painting. Wrapped in their struggle, the man and the angel turn to face the objects of what we know as the real world. These have form, but no meaning. The real is unreal, the unreal is real. Klee reached the heights of his art and achieved the impossible in this work, because in it, he has summed up his message succinctly and with a compassionate farewell for his fellow man.

Exhausted and ill, he was taken to a sanatorium in Orselina-Locarno, above Lago Maggiore, early in 1940, *Italy and death* possibly still hoping for recovery. But his recognition of impending death proved to be correct. On June 8, he was transferred to a clinic in Muralto-Locarno, where he died on June 29 of paralysis of the heart, occasioned by the strain of his skin illness. His body was cremated on July 1, and the urn with his ashes was interred in September, 1942, in the Schosshalden Cemetery in Bern.

On his tombstone, a sentence from his diary is inscribed:

"I cannot be understood in this world, for I am as much at home with the dead as with those yet to be born— a little closer to the heart of creation than is normal, yet still too far away."

ROBERT FISHER

13

NOTES ON THE COLOR PLATES

1. *The Artist's Sister*. 1903. Oil. Bern, Klee Foundation. Painted after his return to Bern from Munich, where he had studied art for three years and after a six month trip to Italy. This is a completely realistic work, and quite skillfully done. Had Klee desired to make his mark in the world of art as a realist, he no doubt could have done so, as he had obviously learned well at the Knirr School and the Munich Academy.

2. *Garden Scene with Watering Can*. 1905. Water color on glass. Bern, Felix Klee Collection. Painting on glass (called *sous verre* because the work is then viewed through the glass), Klee came remarkably near to the style of the Fauvists, about whom he knew nothing at the time. The bright colors remind many viewers of those of Matisse.

3. *Girl with Jugs*. 1910. Oil on panel. Bern, Felix Klee Collection. This, his first oil painting, except for studies done as a student, was accomplished within a few months of seeing eight paintings by Cezanne, the first encounter he was to have with the works of the man he was to admire so much.

4. *Saint Germain*. 1914. Water color. Brussels, Private Collection. A suburb of Tunis, not the quarter of the French capital, is portrayed here. Klee had visited Paris in 1905 and in 1912, and in his examination of the works of other artists, had come to admire deeply the paintings of Corot, Watteau, Rembrandt and Goya. More than these influences, however, had an effect on his own work—the trip to Tunisia in April, 1914, had become in fact a one-way journey into a new era of discovery in the harmony of colors. During this epochal trip to North Africa, Klee for the first time felt himself destined to be an artist, making his memorable remark, "I and color are one." This painting, one of several similar scenes, reflects the artist's determination to make use of his new discovery.

5. *Homage to Picasso*. 1914. Oil on panel. Connecticut, Private Collection. Though Klee felt he was painting in the manner of Picasso

14

here, some would say the only similarity is the oval shape of the work itself. Whether the Cubism of Picasso inspired the squares here or whether the shapes, forerunners of his "magic squares," are simply ancestors to the signs and symbols Klee will develop to their logical end, will have to remain a subject for speculation. The man to whom Klee dedicated this work was not to meet Klee until 1937, when the latter was already seriously ill. At that time, he referred to the Swiss-born artist as "Pascal-Napoleon," a cryptic but flattering evaluation.

6. *The Niesen*. 1915. Water color. Bern, Private Collection. One vivid memory of his trip to Tunisia resulted in this painting, which contains not only more little squares but the first of the Arab-inspired symbols which are to become so popular with the artist. They include the star, the crescent of Islam and the pine tree, somehow transplanted from its European habitat to the dunes of North Africa.

7. *Fabric of a Pigeon's Cote*. 1917. Water color. Stuttgart, Private Collection. From March, 1916, until Armistice Day, 1918, Klee served in the German army, where he tried to paint away from the eyes of his superiors. Finding the time and opportunity, he investigated pure forms, ending up with compositions such as these, in which triangles, balls and blocks are piled one atop the other for their total effect.

8. *View at the North Pole*. 1917. Water color. Zurich, Private Collection. Not intending to paint a landscape, he merely experimented with his beloved rectangles and triangles. When he was finished, the result suggested a polar landscape. When he painted this, he had already become a friend of Rilke, and was possibly influenced by the poet's mystical realism. He also began to sell a few works this year and eagerly awaited his discharge from the army.

9. *There is an Egg*. 1917. Water color. Zurich, Private Collection. Not merely an abstract painting, but reality amidst the jumble of geometrical forms, is the aim of the artist here. "What we see is only a possibility, a suggestion. True reality lies beneath what we see."

10. *Flowery Myth*. 1918. Water color. Hannover, Private Collection. The poetic side of Klee's nature comes to the fore in this kind of

romantic painting, which not only served as an escape mechanism for him while enduring Army boredom, but was also a means of expressing the symbols of his new technique in an appealing manner.

11. *With the Eagle.* 1918. Water color. Bern, Klee Foundation. This painting, resembling a dream world in a formal setting, was done during Klee's Red Period. Under an eye of overpowering authority, Klee indulges in some of his favorite symbols from North Africa—moon, crescent of Islam, Biblical star, oddly-shaped plants, cupolas, little flags, fragments of Arabic script, and the colors of sand and oasis, yellow and green. Not all are shown in *With the Eagle,* but all can be seen in one or another of Klee's paintings.

12. *Once Emerged from the Gray of Night.* 1918. Water color and collage. Bern, Klee Foundation. In this picture-poem, Klee's words (at top) are matched by the colors below, which change to fit each letter. The silver paper in the middle serves as an interval, like the double bar in the poem's second line. This experiment with words, letters and colors will continue for several years (see Plates 20 and 28).

13. *Under a Black Star.* 1918. Oil on muslin. Basel, Richard Doetsch-Benziger Collection. Still in the army, and perhaps suffering from a sense of frustration and uneasiness, he painted this composition, involving not only the Biblical star of Judah but the cross and many suns and moons.

14. *Tree House.* 1918. Water color. Pasadena, Museum of Fine Arts. The oriental and fantastic overtones of this painting may indicate Klee's own escapist mood during the last days of the war. Bordering on sheer fantasy, it pictures a flying fish with wings of a bird, skeletons of trees, and the pine trees themselves, now turned into triangles, as well as the star and moon of previous works.

15. *See the Setting Sun.* 1919. Water color. New York, Private Collection. The sun sets, naturally, in the direction pointed by the arrow. Klee invents for us a house, with cupola roof, delineated only by its two windows and a staircase. This year, during which he is rejected by the Stuttgart Academy, where he applied for a teaching post, is one of intensive self-analysis for the artist.

16. *Villa R.* 1919. Oil. Basel, Museum of Fine Arts. Turning ordinary letters into forms, like triangles or rectangles, was one of Klee's objectives. He was least successful at this when he used large, single letters as in this painting. It is neither archway, building nor appendix—it is just the letter "R", ambiguous and intriguing.

17. *Melting Snows of the North Pole.* 1920. Oil. Bern, Hans Meyer Collection. The mysterious, glowing auras of this painting attract and instill fear. Unlike *View at the North Pole* (Plate 8), this work seems to have been composed with polar ice in mind. Once again, however, reality falls behind fantasy, and we find here another cupola house, built of two windows and a triangle, in which artist and viewer alike can imagine themselves safe from the cold.

18. *Message from an Airborne Fairy.* 1920. Water color and oil. Stuttgart, Private Collection. The spirit of air itself is the theme of this work. The very air we breathe is not what we think we see it to be. That is the message from the visible spirit we see here, in full flight above triangular rooftops.

19. *Doctor Bartolo. Revenge! Oh! Revenge!* 1921. Water color. Switzerland, Private Collection. Turning to different subjects, Klee begins to portray people in his works, fitting them into his craftsmanlike designs. An excellent musician himself and a passionate fan of the opera, Klee here draws the crafty old teacher of music from "The Barber of Seville," by Rossini.

20. *General C's Medals.* 1921. Water color. London, Private Collection. Painted in the shape of the medal itself, this fascinating portrait implies that the general is nothing more than his mouth, and indeed has a name only because of his mouth. Also called *The Order of High C.*

21. *Portrait of a Man in Yellow.* 1921. Water color. Paris, Gallerie Berggruen. The glowing lightning bug of the face is made more imaginative by the absence of heavy lines surrounding it. Painting in two perspectives (the upper forehead looking to the right, the rest of the face to the left) and utilizing a shovel-form as nose and mouth, Klee seems again to want to show us that the mouth is not an integral part of

the body, or to say that it has some kind of inhuman existence of its own.

22. *Perspective of a Room with Inmates.* 1921. Water and oil. Bern, Klee Foundation. Enveloped in the warm camaraderie of the Bauhaus, where the brilliant dialogue between the faculty and students was always sprinkled with wit, Klee deliberately turned this composition into a farce. Seeing the room from all angles, placing its inhabitants, or inmates, on the walls behind lines of perspective, and turning viewer and inmates round and round, Klee has the last laugh.

23. *Woman's Pavilion.* 1921. Oil on panel. New York, Private Collection. A dark building set in the background, with a hint of the convent's cross on its spire, exudes two streams of women, who for all the world could be angels or nuns. Surrounded by rounded trees, which may be people or priests, after all, they form a lane for the viewer to pass through on the way to the Woman's Pavilion.

24. *A Cold, Dead Garden.* 1921. Water color. Basel, Private Collection. The passage of time and a hint of musical composition is intended by Klee, who repeats several objects to give the painting depth and movement. Note the leaf-shaped patterns at top, the rectangles in plane formation below and the ever-present squares to left and right.

25. *Face of a Flower.* 1922. Water color. New York, Private Collection. Everything points downward here, as if into the ground, from which the flower springs. Squatting at the center of several rectangular petals, the flower, legs akimbo, hands folded, shows its amazed face. No doubt it is surprised at having its portrait painted in this manner. This painting is occasionally printed upside down in art books, but the position here is accurate as attested to by Klee's signature, about two-thirds of the way up on the right hand side.

26. *Message of Autumn.* 1922. Water color. Basel, Private Collection. The architectural rhythm of the magic squares, the feeling of light and sun achieved by the gap in the squares, make this a lyrical painting. Klee's knowledge of music and drafting made possible this wonderful blending of the arts.

27. *Mirror of a Silver Moon*. 1922. Water color. Stuttgart, Private Collection. The interplay of line and patches of color, musical in intent, serves to create for the viewer a very special landscape and wistful themes like this one. The simple, silvery moon is reflected into a mirror and is seen as a jumble of every kind of line, plane and fancy figure.

28. *Vocal Fabric of the Singer Rosa Silber*. 1922. Gouache and gesso on canvas. New York, Museum of Modern Art. This representation of the five vowels, the fundamental elements of vocal music, looks like a collage, but isn't. Rosa Silber was a prima donna whom Klee admired greatly from his student days.

29. *Senecio*. 1922. Oil on linen. Basel, Kunstmuseum. A brilliant display of the artist's sense of color, this young lady was born from the marriage of geometry and the color spectrum. Lovely as a field flower, the maiden betrays a knowing eye, making her otherwise innocent mask the more attractive.

30. *Architecture*. 1923. Oil. Bern, Klee Foundation. Aiming to formalize his magic squares, Klee divided his canvas into horizontal and vertical lines and painted an architectural design, using color to express the suggestion of a structure's outline. In this year, he also published "Ways of Studying Nature," in which he analyzed his own attitude towards nature.

31. *Architecture*. 1923. Oil. Bern, Herman Rupf Collection. Subtitled *Piled Yellow and Violet Cubes,* this work was painted in the same year as the one bearing the same title (Plate 30). Klee envisioned his magic squares as being independent units, each having its own life, but nevertheless interdependent with the squares surrounding it. In theory, each square could be a separate picture in itself.

32. *Captured Harlequin*. 1923. Water and oil. U.S.A., Private Collection. Remaining firm in his devotion to form, Klee traps his rare human figure in a geometrical prison. Some of Klee's forms seem to paint themselves, or to occur unconsciously in his pictures. In this, we almost get the feeling that the clown was an afterthought, the accidental result of the progression of rectangles and other forms until the

harlequin's sudden appearance in the center.

33. *Chinese Poetry.* 1923. Water color. Zurich, Private Collection. Never having seen China, and certainly not intending to be caught in the "error" of filling that country with Christian crosses, Klee painted a mythical China which exists nowhere but in his head. That the symbols and forms have no relation to the China we know only proves Klee's point that the world which is visible to us is not the real world. In any event, Klee painted *his* China.

34. *Lagoon City.* 1932. Water color. Bern, Private Collection. This is one of many works which Klee painted after his visit to Venice during this year. The waterways and buildings of that city by the sea are here delineated in a manner which suggests the rhythm of the water, and the music of water and song.

35. *Battle Scene from the Comic Fantastic Opera, "The Seafarer."* 1923. Water color and oil on paper. Basel, Private Collection. A classical composition based on the opera also known as "Sinbad the Sailor," this composition shows us a bitter struggle between marvelous monsters and the sailor under the bright lights of the theater. The magic squares, or their close relatives, weave their splendid pattern through the dark and forbidding sea.

36. *The Weeping Man (Lomolarm).* 1923. Water color. New York, F. C. Shang Collection. Portraying his man with the same shape of face as that given to the flower in *Face of a Flower* (Plate 25), Klee even coins a new word for this mournful visage. *Lomolarm* is his blending of *l'homme aux larmes,* man of tears. His wit, however, is overshadowed by the tragic air of the subject, from whose eyes pour blood-red tears.

37. *Puppet Show.* 1923. Water color. Bern, Klee Foundation. A lover of the stage, Klee enjoyed making masks and puppets for his son, Felix. He also constructed stage settings for the dolls and watched his son try his hand at painting. "The pictures which my little boy Felix paints are often better than mine, because mine have often been filtered through my brain...."

38. *Garden of Birds.* 1924. Water color. Munich, Private Collection. Walking in a gloomy garden, in a light suggesting that at the bottom of the sea, these birds may have been seen in the dim light of a dream. Although he warned against too much study of nature as "a comfortable crutch," Klee could years later remark that nature, "if we love her, will yet lead us into liberty." These views, expressed in his essays, were backed up by his own studies of flora and fauna, revealed in paintings such as this one.

39. *Red Skirt.* 1924. Oil. Bern, Private Collection. ·Dancing wildly, even flying into the air, these participants in a ballet on the stage of Klee's imagination may have been patterned after some favored dance at the Weimar Opera House. During this period of a happy and productive life at the Bauhaus, Klee often indulged his sense of humor to produce whimsical fantasies such as this one.

40. *The Bird Called Pep.* 1925. Water color and oil. Bern, Private Collection. In this charming work, Klee once again played a private little joke, painting the bird to resemble a well-known art dealer, perhaps the owner of the Sturm Gallery. Klee tried to make the surface of the picture fluffy, a technique practiced in etching, and which in music may be likened to a trill. Nothing in music more closely approximates the bird's song than a trill, and Klee was never happier than when trying to marry his favorite arts, painting and music.

41. *Picture of Fish.* 1925. Water color and gouache. Basel, Richard Doetsch-Benziger Collection. Anticipating the forms so much admired by Alexander Calder, this mobile-like presentation illustrates precisely Klee's comment that "in simplicity there can be riches." Klee seemed fascinated with fish all his life, probably because they are the most simple, yet most pliable form of life which can move in a milieu recognizable to man in his everyday routine.

42. *Fish Magic.* 1925. Oil and water color, varnished. Philadelphia, Museum of Art. In an unusually large picture for this period, Klee portrays all manner of disparate objects in a plane fantasy. A picture within a picture. By this time, Klee was beginning to think of himself as a Surrealist, having joined the first exhibition of Surrealist painters

in Paris, along with Picasso, Miro, Arp and Max Ernst.

43. *Small Dunes.* 1926. Oil. New York, Private Collection. An island beach is here shown with the individual colors of the sand and plants magnified as under a prism and shown to us separately, and, as intended, simply. The rhythm of the plants at the bottom is set off by the punctuation and crests of those at left and right, meeting in an overall wave of music at the top. A masterful piece of art.

44. *Chosen Site.* 1927. Water color and pen. Berlin, Theodor Werner Collection. The relation of cities to the sky, toward which the buildings are thrust by man, occupied Klee for some time as he traveled about Italy and Corsica during this year. A mysterious moon broods over an ideal city, each reflecting the other in their criss-crossed lines which just accidentally happen to form squares.

45. *City on Two Hills.* 1927. Water color and pen on cardboard. Stuttgart, Max Fischer Collection. Similar to *Chosen Site,* but without the wondrous moon, this is a dream town made from lines. The actual image, capable of being seen by a man intrigued with reality, is quite close to the city which Klee envisions in his mind. This happy coincidence of "reality" with the artist's vision does not occur too often.

46. *The Ships Depart.* 1927. Oil. Bern, Private Collection. Cast onto a dark and forbidding sea, the ships nevertheless can be seen as symbols of free movement, heading out to the open sea of liberty in the direction of the arrow. Moving from some kind of a restricted past into an unpredictable but virile adventure, the ships may very well represent the artist's own feelings of the future during these successful days.

47. *Prospect.* 1927. Water color and oil. New York, Private Collection. Some buildings are drawn in perspective, some are not, causing the entire town to fall into a kind of imbalance which creates its own sense of balance. Several of Klee's works resulting from his trip to Corsica during this year are topped off by little flags of the type shown here.

48. *She Howls and We Play.* 1928. Oil. Bern, Klee Foundation. Nearly all Klee's works were given their titles after the actual painting

was completed. The title here shows how a painting can grow to express itself in an almost accidental way, more or less suggesting a title to the artist when he settles back to see what his finished product looks like. This kind of attitude may also suggest why titles are frequently of no use at all for some paintings. Klee's constant preoccupation with fantasy and dreams may have had much to do with this painting and, subsequently, with its odd title.

49. *Clouds Above a Ball.* 1928. Water color. Bern, Felix Klee Collection. A mild demonstration of Klee's idea that only by distorting natural forms can nature be reborn is apparent here. With a few horizontal and perpendicular lines and only a bit of perspective, Klee here is able to achieve the impression of an enormous space.

50. *Old Town and Bridge.* 1928. Tempera. Basel, Richard Doetsch-Benziger Collection. Simple forms repeated over and over make this horizontal frieze-like work a delight to the eye. Its order and formality make an enchanting picture, especially when combined with Klee's favorite symbols, the pine, triangles, and so forth, without which we would feel the composition incomplete. During 1928, Klee visited France and also published his "Exact Experiments in the Realm of Art." His comments in that essay are supported by his work, in this picture even more than in many others.

51. *Cat with Bird.* 1928. Oil. New York, Private Collection. In this allegorical portrayal of enemies at peace, Klee places a moon to balance the cat's eyes and nose. In so doing, and by placing the bird on the forehead of the cat, he has lent an air of oriental mystery to the composition. Again, however, though the cat was Klee's favorite animal, he did not consciously intend to portray a cat. He merely painted lines, circles and shades of color and found the cat had entered the picture.

52. *Clown.* 1929. Chalk and oil. St. Louis, Private Collection. This Don Quixote-like portrayal of a noble and humorous clown is one of Klee's most famous works. Now 50 years old, Klee found that he was required to formulate his ideas for the benefit of his students. Accordingly, he became slightly stylized in his own works; the more he thought about his painting, the less he experimented.

53. *Uncomposed Objects in Space.* 1929. Water color. Switzerland, Private Collection. Klee's attitude toward perspective is shown here. If you must have perspective, he seems to say, why then, make it obvious. He aimed always to astonish, and he achieves that objective here.

54. *Six Types.* 1930. Water color and gouache. Bern, Felix Klee Collection. When Klee added colors and tones to his scramble of abstract and geometrical lines, they leaped into life. He always experimented with materials. Frequently mixing oils and water colors, chalk and Chinese ink, he complained now and then that he didn't know whether a certain painting was an oil or a water color.

55. *Hovering (About to Take off).* 1930. Oil. Bern, Klee Foundation. Using his lightest and brightest color just below the arrowhead, Klee hopes to create a sense of great, swirling activity and then to direct the viewer to the ascent. This composition seems to reflect some of Klee's revolutionary ideas about the technique of Divisionism, which had been invented by Seurat in the 1880's.

56. *Individualized Measurement of Strata.* 1930. Pastel on paste background. Bern, Klee Foundation. Klee's trip to Egypt in 1929 is reflected in this simultaneous expression of nature and history (space and time) in a rhythmical arrangement of tones.

57. *Outside, Life is Gay.* 1931. Water color. Switzerland, Private Collection. Again working in the manner of the Divisionists, Klee suggests here the mosaic work he saw during his trips to Italy and Tunisia. During the 1930–33 period, Klee also adapted the techniques of making stained glass to his works, reminding us of his earlier attempts to paint *sous verre* (see Pl. 2).

58. *Diana.* 1931. Oil. New York, Private Collection. Using dots in a different manner than Seurat, Klee tries to show shades of light and intensity dot by dot, instead of merely relying on the overall effect achieved through the use of dots. This homage to the Roman goddess of the moon is appropriate to Klee, the man who could never forego his attraction to all things lunar. The eye in the arrow is no part of the Roman legend, and probably reflects the artist's love of North African

mystery and symbolism.

59. *Ad Parnassum*. 1932. Oil. Bern, Kunstmuseum. Again employing the mosaic technique, Klee appears to be following the Divisionist school in a totally devoted manner. He is more influenced by mosaic, however, than by any loyalty to a doctrine, as he feels mosaic can better express his drive to portray the intensity of eternal light.

60. *Garden Gate M.* 1932. Oil and gouache. Basel, Richard Doetsch-Benziger Collection. Klee loved to use the alphabet to amuse and bemuse, not only because of his sense of humor, but because of his continuing interest in hieroglyphics, symbols and signs.

61. *Two Friends Strolling Down a Road*. 1938. Water color. Basel, Richard Doetsch-Benziger Collection. Painted during one of his most prolific years, and in his beloved Bern, this work shows Klee's preoccupation with color in his later years. The two people, however, seem to be isolated from the immense world around them. This is perhaps an expression of Klee's sadness during his years of illness.

62. *While Dropping Anchor*. 1932. Oil. St. Louis, Private Collection. The moon glows weakly over this watery nocturnal scene so reminiscent of Seurat's seascapes. The ship is suggested with simple lines, but it already seems on the verge of destruction in the dispersed light of the dots.

63. *Scholar*. 1933. Water color. Bern, Private Collection. Painted during the year in which he was forced to leave Germany after being attacked by the Nazis for his "decadence," this expressed Klee's despair of events in his adopted land.

64. *Reposing Sphinx*. 1934. Oil on canvas. Bern, Klee Foundation. Whether an accident or a conscious reminder of his visit to Egypt, this picture shows Klee, the optimist. Impressed by Egypt's sand and oases, he usually painted that country in terms of yellows and greens. The blue used here, especially alongside the face of the sphinx, may represent the Nile, however. The colors are tranquil, despite the central mystery.

65. *The Creator*. 1934. Oil. Bern, Klee Foundation. Grotesque

progenitor of all things, the creator is seen in a bizarre dance which is at first glance merely charming, but on closer examination hardly trivial. Klee's odd affinity for the grotesque is expressed in parallel lines, the linear form least likely to be considered evil.

66. *Untamed Waters.* 1934. Water color. Bern, Private Collection. This shows Klee's attempts to portray "infinite movement" and is remarkably similar in concept, but not in style, to the studies of Leonardo da Vinci of the force of water power. In Leonardo's series, "The Deluge," in which the world is destroyed by water, the force of the swirling masses is explosive in nature. Klee, however, adds a light touch to the painting by including some pink, hardly a color of destruction, alleviating the turgid streams of blue.

67. *Spirits Leaving the Body.* 1934. Water color. Bern, Private Collection. To some degree reflecting his anguish at being expelled from his beloved Germany, and his unhappy return to Switzerland, this work and *Fear* are deeply disturbing. Klee's memories of Egypt are included in this work, through the use of pyramids, mummy-like objects and the symbols of his own North African obsession.

68. *Fear.* 1934. Water color. U.S.A., Private Collection. The complicated reality of fear is here expressed by the oppression of a huge, monstrous power, bearing down on and surrounding a small, newly-born form of life (probably a fish).

69. *Dame Demon.* 1935. Bern, Klee Foundation. Even though this year marked the appearance of the disease which was to kill him (scleroderma, a hardening of the skin tissues), Klee expresses the devil in a bright and gay form, as a lady. Goethe did the same in Mephistopheles' transformation in "Faust." In this period, he approaches the work of Picasso to a small degree, but Surrealism holds no attraction for Klee and he soon leaves his flirtation with it behind.

70. *Picture Page.* 1937. Oil on panel. Washington, Phillips Gallery. Several arcs are invited to join in this composition, which relies heavily on Klee's infatuation with Arabic symbols and his memories of Egypt and Tunisia. After producing little during 1936 because of illness, Klee

returned to work in earnest in 1937.

71. *View of a Stage*. 1937. Pastel. Bern, Private Collection. Klee's fascination with the theater continued until his death. He began to use signs or symbols which he felt had quasi-semantic value, like Chinese ideographs. Many seem to have Islamic connotations. In 1937 and 1938, he used black and bold simple lines repeatedly (Plates 71 through 78).

72. *Red Waistcoat*. 1938. Gouache and charcoal. New York, F.C. Shang Collection. More symbols or signs appear here, and as Klee paints increasingly large canvases in 1937 and 1938, he renews his courage in his art. As in a game of hide-and-go-seek, the man in the red waistcoat and the animals suggested by the lines around him are nearly lost to the observer.

73. *Fruits on Blue*. 1938. Color in paste medium on panel. Bern, Klee Foundation. Klee's determination to maintain his searching outlook is evident in this magnificent achievement, painted despite his illness. The bright blue of this work seems to suggest the Mediterranean, which Klee no doubt longed to see once again.

74. *Park near L.* 1938. Oil. Bern, Klee Foundation. Klee no doubt visited this park near Lucerne on his frequent rides in an open carriage, which continued until 1939. Klee seems to suggest with these delicate colors and graceful forms a kind of poetic world in which he sought relief from pain in these last years of his life. This is one of his most appealing and charming works.

75. *Oriental Lusciousness*. 1938. Oil. New York, Private Collection. The mysterious moon of Klee's desires shines as luminously as ever over this collection of Egyptian colors. The warm carpet of color, while hardly Oriental, is distinctly Arabic in inspiration. As so many do, Klee confused the Orient of Iraq and Syria with the North African Arab culture of Tunisia and Egypt.

76. *Blue Eyed Fish*. 1938. Oil. Basel, Richard Doetsch-Benziger Collection. Bluer than the blue of the Mediterranean, the background sets off the dark eyes, allowing them to stand out clearly and causing the

artist's beloved fish to appear somewhat sinister.

77. *Azure Fruit.* 1938. Color in paste medium. Bern, Klee Foundation. Less firmly sketched than the lines in *Fruits on Blue,* the lines here are tentative and the color is only casually painted in. Nevertheless, this vigorous work is just as strong as *Fruits on Blue.* Here, Klee tried to express his vision of nature in the simplest terms.

78. *Intention.* 1938. Bern, Klee Foundation. Man, animals, trees are all suggested here, yet Klee is obviously more interested in the hieroglyphic aspect of the composition than anything else. Note the truncated and distorted pine tree, which has been with Klee from his youth.

79. *La Belle Jardinière.* 1939. Oil and tempera. Bern, Klee Foundation. Exhausted by his illness, Klee spent a great deal of time on the shore of a lake near Bern, hoping to regain his health. The woman gardening seems to symbolize grief or passion, suffusing a green garden with the reds of death, the blue of fear and the speckled, motley tones of uncertainty.

80. *Insula Dulcamara.* 1938. Oil. Bern, Klee Foundation. Nowhere do symbols and space blend more beautifully than in this large painting of an island which had haunted Klee for years. Existing in its own ethereal spring, this dream island seems to defy time, and in so doing, to defy the possibility of death.

81. *Intoxication.* 1939. Water and oil. Bern, Hans Meyer Collection. Klee's objective in 1919, to render visible what lies secreted beyond the world of sight, was unchanged in 1939, when he painted this composition. Impossible to explain, this work is typical of Klee's coming to terms with symbols and meanings beyond the point where man's language is capable of definition.

82. *Stern Visage.* 1939. Water color and tempera. Bern, Klee Foundation. A ghost, perhaps derived from Klee's dreams, appears not so much to frighten as to suggest a familiarity. Knowing his impending death, Klee perhaps decided to draw its face, waiting behind an innocent

facade.

83. *Flower in a Stone.* 1939. Oil. Lausanne, Cantonal Fine Arts Museum. Like the circle, which never ends, the cross, which always denotes a site, and a triangle, the sign of mystery, these symbols are flowers which will never die. Further encased in a stone, they are unreachable and ever-lasting. Klee's preoccupation with death and his envy for the perennial flower, the epitome of reincarnation, is obvious here.

84. *Woodlouse in Enclosure.* 1940. Pastel. Bern, Klee Foundation. Too big to move about freely, the woodlouse is frustrated and annoyed. Klee's humor is nearly lost here in the implications of what he was trying to express. Perhaps Klee felt like a woodlouse, grown too big in the small world of his experience, trapped and eager to get out. Trapped also by the fear of death, he seeks liberation from the mortal binding which surrounds us all.

85. *Woman in National Costume.* 1940. Gouache. Bern, Klee Foundation. A stained glass picture, this figure's appeal seems nearly religious in nature. Traces of the same love for black lines favored by Rouault, the large patches of color which Van Gogh liked and the surrealism of Picasso are all visible here.

86. *Tall Standing Aborigine.* 1940. Oil and charcoal. Bern, Klee Foundation. Mystery is supplied by the blue tones, but Klee's overall fascination with Africa, with its primitive attributes and its symbols, is the most obvious impression created by this work.

87. *Dark Journey.* 1940. Bern, Felix Klee Collection. These abstract symbols express the dark journey to death more realistically than photographs. His triangles, moons and dots, his arcs and patches of solid color have suddenly, without warning, metamorphosed from charming landscapes into grinning monsters of death.

88. *Double.* 1940. Color in paste medium. Bern, Klee Foundation. The title refers to life and death, the double existence of men, and in this painting, Klee seems to be portraying the world which lies between. His brave attempt to wield the brighter brush of a happier day is belied

by the grim appearance of his shapes.

89. *Drummer*. 1940. Gouache. Bern, Klee Foundation. This extremely simple venture into calligraphy has produced an almost amoeba-like form, springing from a white jelly into the blood-spattered realities of life. His lines approach modern Japanese calligraphy.

90. *Death and Fire*. 1940. Oil. Bern, Klee Foundation. Hinting at an African adventure and beyond that, at the mysteries of the Arab world, this strikes the viewer in a particularly ominous way. A dreadful moon shines down on the grinning mask of death, but man, as irrepressible as was Klee himself, strides beyond death toward the fire and the moon, unafraid.

91. *Still Life*. 1940. Oil. Bern, Felix Klee Collection. Klee's last work, with his mystical moon and the story of the struggle of Jacob and the Angel, at lower left. The latter symbolizes the world beyond, just as the juxtaposition of familiar objects surrounding it refers to our preoccupation with the world as we see it and as we think it really is.

PAUL KLEE

1879   Born on December 18 at Münchenbuchsee, near Bern, son of a German teacher and Swiss mother. Family moves to Bern in 1880.

1886–98   Attends primary and high school in Bern, also learning to play the violin from the age of seven.

1898   Goes to Munich in October, where he enters the Knirr School of Art.

1900   In October, enters the Munich Academy, where he studies anatomy, etching and art history. Joins the studio of Franz Stuck.

1901   Visits Italy for six months.

1903–05   Produces his first etchings and serves in the Bern Symphony Orchestra as a violinist.

1905   Visits Paris briefly.

1906   Exhibits a few etchings in Munich, and in April travels to Berlin. In September, marries Lily Stumpf and in October, settles in Munich.

1907   His only child, Felix, is born.

1908   Refused membership in a Munich artists' association, but is employed for a few months by the Debschitz Art School.

31

1909	Some of his works exhibited at the Berlin Sezession.
1910	More than fifty of his drawings, paintings and sketches are shown at the Bern Museum, Zurich and Winterthur.
1911	After two years of work, finishes his illustrations to *Candide*, and helps found Sema, an organization of artists including Kubin and Scharff. Meets Kandinsky, Franz Marc and Hans Arp.
1912	Joins in the second exhibition of the Blaue Reiter, a group organized by Kandinsky and Marc. In April, visits Paris.
1913	Klee's works are shown in the Sturm Gallery, Berlin.
1914	Helps organize the New Munich Sezession. Visits Tunisia in April, and comes to recognize the importance of color.
1916	Shortly after his friend Franz Marc is killed at Verdun, Klee is conscripted into the German Army (March 11).
1917	The Sturm Gallery sells several of his works.
1918	About Christmas time, Klee is demobilized. Returns to Munich.
1919	Rejected by the Stuttgart Academy as a teacher, but begins to sell his pictures and publish his theories.
1920	Exhibits nearly 400 works in Munich. *Candide* illustrations published. His own significant essay, "Creative Confessions," is published in the *Tribüne der Kunst und Zeit*.

1921	Leaves Munich for Weimar, where he becomes a professor at the Bauhaus. Publishes his monograph "Kairuan (The History of Klee and the Art of our Time)."
1922	Joins in exhibits in Berlin and Wiesbaden.
1923	Publishes "Ways of Studying Nature" and exhibits again in Berlin.
1924	Founds the Blauen Vier group in Weimar with Kandinsky, Feininger and Jawlensky. Lectures "On Modern Art" in Jena and makes a brief trip to Sicily. The first exhibition of his works in the USA held in New York.
1925	When the Bauhaus is forced to leave Weimar, Klee moves with the faculty and students to Dessau. Exhibits again in Munich and joins exhibition of Surrealists in Paris, along with Picasso, Miro, Arp and Max Ernst. First one-man exhibition in Paris. Publishes "Pedagogical Sketches."
1926	Visits Italy again.
1928	Publishes "Exact Experiments in the Realm of Art" and visits northern France. In December, visits Egypt on a grant from a Brunswick art collector.
1929	Returns to Dessau, visits France and Spain. On his fiftieth birthday a large exhibition is organized in Berlin and he is also shown in Paris.
1930	Exhibitions in New York (Museum of Modern Art) and Berlin.

1931	In April, resigns from the Bauhaus and goes to teach at the Düsseldorf Academy.
1933	After returning to Germany from a short trip to France, Klee is severely attacked by the Nazis as a degenerate artist, and is dismissed from the Düsseldorf Academy under political pressure. Around Christmas, leaves Germany forever and returns to Bern, where his sister still living.
1934	The first Klee exhibition in England is held in London. In Germany, a book of his drawings is confiscated by the Nazis.
1935	A large exhibit is held in Bern. The first symptoms appear of the disease that will finally kill him.
1937	Resumes work after treatment for his illness for nearly a year. Exchanges visits with Picasso, Braque and Kandinsky. After confiscating over 100 of his works from public galleries and auctioning them off, the Nazis include 17 works in their exhibit of "degenerate art" in Munich and other German cities.
1939	Despite increasing illness, he paints prolifically, producing some of his greatest works.
1940	After a large exhibit in Bern and the death of his father, Klee enters a sanatorium near Locarno on May 10. On June 8, he is moved to a clinic at Muralto-Locarno, where he dies on June 29 of paralysis of the heart, occasioned by the strain of his illness, scleroderma. On July 1, his body is cremated, but it is not until September, 1942 that his ashes are interred in the Schosshalden Cemetery in Bern.

LIST OF COLOR PLATES

THE PLATES

1 *The Artist's Sister*. 1903. Oil. 11½″ × 13¼″. Bern, Klee Foundation. At the age of 24, Klee painted this conventional but sensitive portrait.

2 *Garden Scene with Watering Can.* 1905. Water color on glass. 5″ × 7″. Bern, Felix Klee Collection. An early experimental work, painted on glass and meant to be seen through glass.

3 *Girl with Jugs.* 1910. Oil on panel. 13¾″ × 10⅝″. Bern, Felix Klee Collection. Perhaps done under the influence of Cézanne, whose use of blue is recalled here.

4 *Saint Germain*. 1914. Water color. $7\frac{7}{8}'' \times 10\frac{1}{4}''$. Brussels, Private Collection. One of several similar scenes painted during this momentous year in Klee's life.

5 *Homage to Picasso*. 1914. Oil on panel. 15″ × 11⅝″. Connecticut, Private Collection. Klee may have thought this was in a style similar to Picasso's, but it remains quite personal.

1915 250 Der Niesen

6 *The Niesen.* 1915. Water color. 7⅛″ × 10″. Bern, Private Collection. His use of luminous color here results directly from his African trip.

7 *Fabric of a Pigeon's Cote.* 1917. Water color. $8\frac{7}{8}'' \times 6\frac{1}{4}''$. Bern, Private Collection. A strongly geometric construction inspired by Cubism.

1917 55.

8   *View at the North Pole.*   1917. Water color. 6¾″×4½″.   Zurich, Private Collection.   One of the works that Klee found time to paint surreptitiously while serving in the army.

9 *There is an Egg.* 1917. Water color. 9⅜" × 6". Zurich, Private Collection. Not merely an abstract painting, but reality amid the jumble of geometric forms was Klee's goal.

10 *Flowery Myth*. 1918. Water color. 12″×6⅞″. Hannover, Private Collection. A work done in Klee's Red Period and clearly inspired by his trip to Tunisia.

11 *With the Eagle*. 1918. Water color. 6¾″×10″. Bern, Klee Foundation. It is remarkable how many of the symbols will recur twenty years later (see Plate 78).

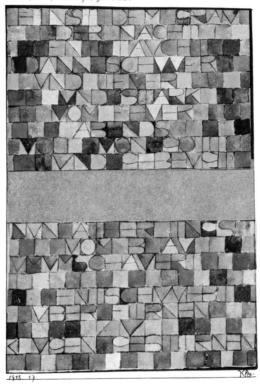

12   *Once Emerged from the Gray of Night.*   1918. Water color and collage. 10″ × 6⅛″.   Bern, Klee
Foundation.   A picture poem in which the verbal and the visual are finely balanced.

13 *Under a Black Star*. 1918. Oil on muslin. 9¼″ × 6¼″. Basel, Richard Doetsch-Benziger Collection. A work abounding in cosmic and religious symbols.

14 *Tree House*. 1918. Water color. 9⅝″×7⅞″. Pasadena, Museum of Fine Arts. The oriental and fantastic overtones indicate Klee's own escapist mood at war's end.

15 *See the Setting Sun.* 1919. Water color. 8″×10⅜″. New York, Private Collection. The arrow, later a favorite sign, already serves here to indicate energy as well as direction.

16 *Villa R.* 1919. Oil. 10⅛″×8¾″. Basel, Museum of Fine Arts. Although inspired by Cubism, the isolated letter here plays a more evocative role.

17 *Melting Snows of the North Pole.* 1920. Oil. 20¾″ × 20¼″. Bern, Hans Meyer Collection. Reminiscent of Kandinsky and Marc in its visionary attitude toward nature.

18 *Message from an Airborne Fairy.* 1920. Water color and oil. 8¾″ × 12¼″. Stuttgart, Private
Collection. Around 1920 Klee perfected his famous linear style and fantastic imagery.

19 *Doctor Bartolo. Revenge! Oh! Revenge!* 1921. Water color. 9½″ × 12¼″. Switzerland, Private Collection. A mock-tragic farce based on Rossini's "Barber of Seville."

20 *General C's Medals*. 1921. Water color. 12½″ × 8¾″. London, Private Collection. An ironical look at the most common design, the alphabet.

61

Portrait of a Man in Yellow.
1921. Water color. 17⅜″ ×
13¾″. Paris, Gallerie Berg-
ruen. One of the few
works in which the presence
of a specific personality is
felt.

22 *Perspective of a Room with Inmates.* 1921. Water and oil. 19⅛″ × 12½″. Bern, Klee Foundation.
The familiar perspective grid is reversed, near and far, inside and out, comically confused.

23 *Woman's Pavilion.* 1921. Oil on Panel. 15¾″ × 20¼″. New York, Private Collection. A haunting, surrealist scene with people and trees inextricably intertwined.

24 *A Cold Dead Garden.* 1921. Water color. 9½″×12″. Basel, Private Collection. One of the earliest fugue-like compositions, where shapes are adumbrated through repetition.

25 *Face of a Flower*. 1922. Water color. 13¾″×8¼″. New York, Private Collection. His favorite African symbols—pine tree, crescent, moon and sun.

26 *Message of Autumn.* 1922. Water color. 9½″×12″. Basel, Private Collection. The choice of colors and a few suggestive shapes transform this geometry into an evocative statement.

27 *Mirror of a Silver Moon.* 1922. Water color. 18⅝"×12". Stuttgart, Private Collection. Compare the similar, but much bolder and less intricate *Diana* of 1931 (Plate 58).

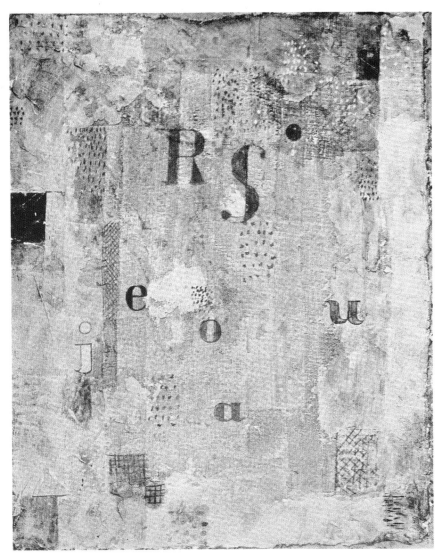

28 *Vocal Fabric of the Singer Rosa Silber*. 1922. Gouache and gesso on canvas. 21″ × 16¼″. New York, Museum of Modern Art. A tribute to a singer in five wittily placed vowels.

29 *Senecio*. 1922. Oil on linen. 16″×15″. Basel, Kunstmuseum. One of the most widely-known of Klee's works is this portrait of a young girl.

30 *Architecture.* 1923. Oil. Bern, Klee Foundation. Far from being an exercise in geometry, this pattern has magical and mystical overtones.

31 *Architecture.* 1923. Oil. 22¼″ × 14½″. Bern, Herman Rupp Collection. Subtitled *Piled Yellow and Violet Cubes.* Toward the top a flat abstract pattern suddenly becomes a moonlit cityscape.

32 *Captured Harlequin*. 1923. Water and oil. 17⅞″×11¾″. U.S.A., Private Collection. A variation on the "fugue" patterns of a few years earlier.

33 *Chinese Poetry*. 1923. Water color. 11¼″×14½″. Zurich, Private Collection. Certain symbols keep recurring—the domes of North Africa, the bird, sun and moon.

34 *Lagoon City*. 1932. Water color. 19¼″ × 11½″. Bern, Private Collection. Upon visiting Venice in 1932 Klee visualized the city in his own way.

35 *Battle Scene from the Comic Fantastic Opera, "The Seafarer."* 1923. Water color and oil on paper. 15″×20⅜″.   Basel, Private Collection.   A brilliant imitation of theatrical lighting and action.

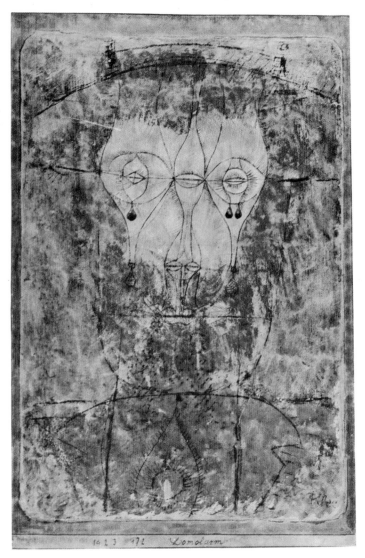

36 *The Weeping Man (Lomolarm).* 1923. Water color. 13¼″ × 9″. New York, F. C. Shang Collection. The intricate linear patterns and expressionist content recall Klee's early work.

37 *Puppet Show*. 1923. Water color. 20⅜″ × 14⅜″. Bern, Klee Foundation. "The pictures which my little boy Felix paints are often better than mine..."

38 *Garden of Birds*. 1924. Water color. $10\frac{1}{2}'' \times 15\frac{3}{8}''$. Munich, Private Collection. A whimsically primitive scene that the Douanier Rousseau would have enjoyed.

39 *Red Skirt*. 1924. Oil. 13¾″×16⅞″. Bern, Private Collection. A basically Cubist composition, but thoroughly transformed by Klee's fantasy.

40 *The Bird Called Pep*. 1925. Water color and oil. 12⅜″×15⅜″. Bern, Private Collection. The bird allegedly resembled a well-known Berlin art dealer.

41 *Picture of Fish*. 1925. Water color and gouache. 24¾″×16⅛″. Basel, Richard Doetsch-Benziger Collection. Klee proves his own comment, "In simplicity there can be riches."

42 *Fish Magic*. 1925. Oil and water color, varnished. 30¼″ × 38⅝″. Philadelphia, Museum of Art.
An intentionally scattered, whimsical arrangement, at once knowing and innocent.

43 *Small Dunes*. 1926. Oil. 14″×9½″. New York, F. C. Shang Collection. The individual colors
of sand and plants are exaggerated as if seen under a prism.

44 *Chosen Site*. 1927. Water color and pen. 18⅛″×12″. Berlin, Theodor Werner Collection. The fascination with cities as fanciful constructions is typical.

45 *City on Two Hills*. 1927. Water color and pen on cardboard. 10″×14″. Stuttgart, Max Fischer Collection. Again Klee remarkably transforms an abstract construction into a poetic image.

46 *The Ships Depart.* 1927. Oil. 19⅝″×23⅝″. Bern, Private Collection. The ships take form as grinning onlookers, private devils to artist and viewer.

47 *Prospect*. 1927. Water color and oil. 12⅜″ × 9½″. New York, Private Collection. After his trip to Corsica, several of his works were flag-bedecked.

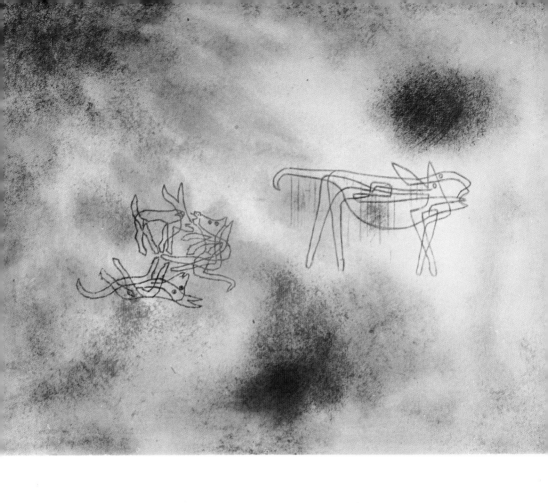

48 *She Howls and We Play.* 1928. Oil. 17⅜″ × 22⅜″. Bern, Klee Foundation. An attempt, typical of Klee, to recapture the simple attitudes of childhood.

49 *Clouds Above a Ball*. 1928. Water color. 12⅛″ × 18″. Bern, Felix Klee Collection. An interesting
juxtaposition of open and closed, vividly painted and delicately drawn forms.

50 *Old Town and Bridge.* 1928. Tempera. 4½″×16¾″. Basel, Richard Doetsch-Benziger Collection. The rough burlap weave is allowed to show through, recalling a tile or mosaic mural.

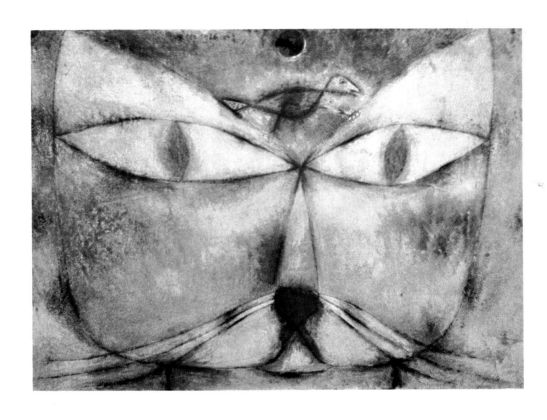

51 *Cat with Bird.* 1928. Oil. 14¾″ × 21⅛″. New York, Private Collection. In this allegory, the
prey appears trapped within the hunter's mind.

52 *Clown.* 1929. Chalk and oil. 26¾″ × 19⅝″. St. Louis, Private Collection. The influence of Picasso's Cubist frontal-profile heads is seen here.

53 *Uncomposed Objects in Space.* 1929. Water color. 12½″×9½″. Switzerland, Private Collection.
A playful comment on Renaissance perspective constructions.

54 *Six Types*. 1930. Water color and gouache. 11⅝″×18⅝″. Bern, Felix Klee Collection. A collection of objects much like those designed by Klee's colleagues at the Bauhaus.

55 *Hovering (About to Take off)*. 1930. Oil. 33″×33″. Bern, Klee Foundation. An ingenious linear design recalling Klee's earlier studies in perspective.

56 *Individualized Measurement of Strata.* 1930. Pastel on paste background. 19″×14″. Bern, Klee Foundation.   Klee's Egyptian trip is reflected in this brilliant array of colors.

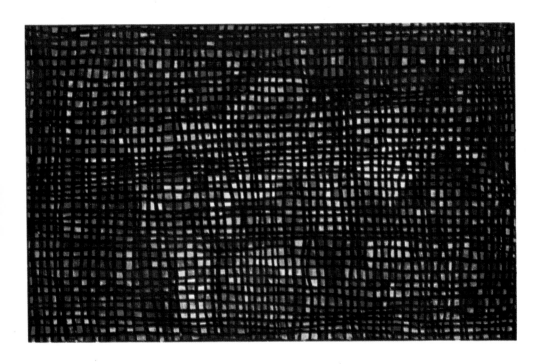

57 *Outside, Life is Gay.* 1931. Water color. 12⅜″ × 19⅜″. Switzerland, Private Collection. Somewhat similar to his *sous verre* works of 1905-06.

58 *Diana.* 1931. Oil. 31½″ × 23⅝″. New York, Private Collection. The Roman goddess of the moon, a natural choice for Klee, who introduced the moon repeatedly into his works.

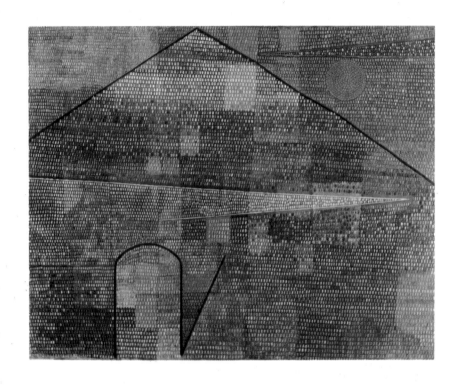

59 *Ad Parnassum*. 1932. Oil. 15½″×19⅝″. Bern, Kunstmuseum. Klee redefines another classical subject, the Greek mountain sacred to Apollo and the Muses.

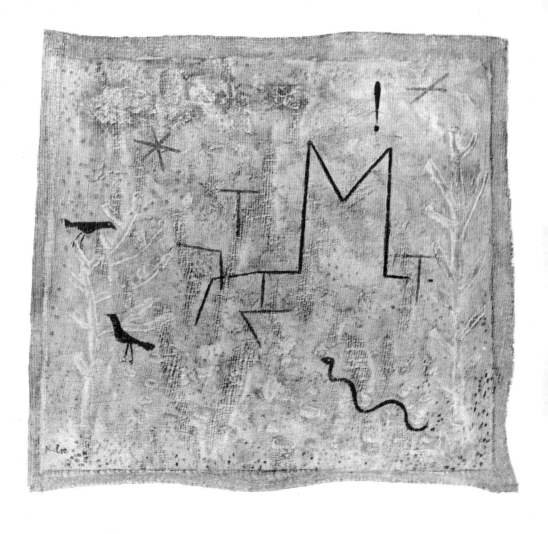

60 *Garden Gate M*. 1932. Oil and gouache. 11¾″ × 13¼″. Basel, Richard Doetsch-Benziger Collection. The pedestrian letter becomes a gate, and is shocked by its own antics.

61 *Two Friends Strolling down a Road.* 1938. Water color. 12⅝″ × 19¼″. Basel, Richard Doetsch-Benziger Col. An old German Romantic theme, figures absorbed in a mysterious landscape.

62 *While Dropping Anchor.* 1932. Oil. 34⅝″×37″. St. Louis, Private Collection. One of many works in which Klee painstakingly reproduces the effect of a mosaic floor.

63 *Scholar*. 1933. Water color. 14″ × 10⅜″. Bern, Private Collection. Another technical experiment with textures, here clearly contrasted with incisive black lines.

64 *Reposing Sphinx.* 1934. Oil on canvas. $37\frac{5}{8}'' \times 47\frac{5}{8}''$. Bern, Klee Foundation. This enigmatic design is as intriguing as its nominal subject.

65   *The Creator*.   1935.   Oil.   16⅞″ × 21¼″.   Bern, Klee Foundation.   The progenitor of all things earthly and spiritual is seen by Klee in a macabre dance.

66 *Untamed Waters.* 1934. Water color. 11½″×19⅝″. Bern, Private Collection. This remarkable work shows to some degree what Klee meant by "movement at rest."

67 *Spirits Leaving the Body.* 1934. Water color. 12¼″×19⅝″. Bern, Private Collection. This may reflect the suffering caused by his expulsion from Germany.

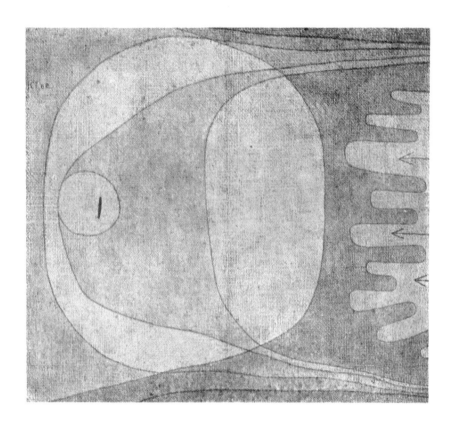

68 *Fear*. 1934. Water color. 19⅝″ × 23⅝″. U.S.A., Private Collection. Klee resolved some of his earlier doubts about his compositions but clearly remained depressed.

69 *Dame Demon*. 1935. 59⅜″ × 39¾″. Bern, Klee Foundation. Though increasingly ill, Klee turned to brighter and more piercing colors in his final years.

70 *Picture Page.* 1937. Oil on panel. 23¼″×22″. Washington, Phillips Gallery. Fascinated by the primitiveness of early woodcut illustrations, Klee shaped this to appear like a woodblock.

71 *View of a Stage*. 1937. Pastel. 22¾″ × 37⅞″. Bern, Private Collection. The effects of transparency
and overlapping here recall Klee's earlier study of Cubism.

72 *Red Waistcoat.* 1938. Gouache and charcoal. 25½″ × 16¾″. New York, F.C. Shang Collection.
The expansive, simplified linear pattern characteristic of his last phase begins to appear.

73 *Fruits on Blue.* 1938. Color in paste medium on panel. $21\frac{5}{8}'' \times 53\frac{1}{2}''$. Bern, Klee Foundation. A work glowing with certainty of purpose, this is one of the artist's largest.

74 *Park near L.* 1939. Oil. 39¼″ × 27½″. Bern, Klee Foundation. "L" stands for Lucerne, and the park was probably one Klee visited often.

75 *Oriental Lusciousness.* 1938. Oil. 19⅝″ × 25⅞″. New York, Private Collection. The colors of Egypt's sky, sand and water are reflected mysteriously here.

76 *Blue Eyed Fish*. 1939. Oil. 5″ × 9½″. Basel, Richard Doetsch-Benziger Collection. By staining, rather than painting opaquely, on rough hemp, Klee achieves both texture and luminosity.

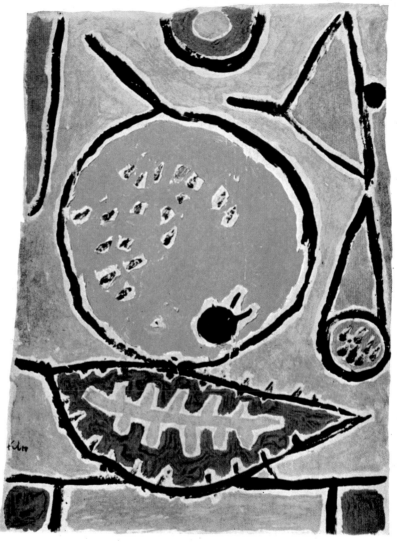

77 *Azure Fruit*. 1938. Color in paste medium. 14⅛″×10⅝″. Bern, Klee Foundation. The lines here are much less firmly drawn than in *Fruits on Blue* (Plate 73).

78 *Intention.* 1938. 30″ × 44⅜″. Bern, Klee Foundation. Traces of Klee's beloved signs and symbols, including an eye, an animal, and a pine tree, are much in evidence.

79　*La Belle Jardinière*.　1939.　Oil and tempera. $37\frac{3}{4}'' \times 27\frac{1}{2}''$.　Bern, Klee Foundation.　The deeply suffused colors give an ominous aspect to a traditionally light-hearted theme.

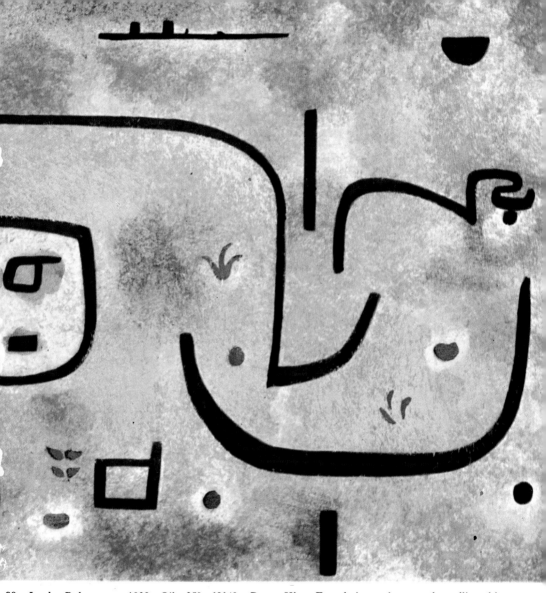

80 *Insula Dulcamara*. 1938. Oil. 35″ × 69¼″. Bern, Klee Foundation. A strongly calligraphic design heralding the linear abstractions of Klee's last years.

81 *Intoxication.* 1939. Water color and oil. 25½″ × 31½″. Bern, Hans Meyer Collection. One of Klee's many technical experiments, here combining water color and oil on unprimed canvas.

82 *Stern Visage.* 1939. Water color and tempera. 12¾″ × 8¼″. Bern, Klee Foundation. A haunting image, at once sinister and humorous.

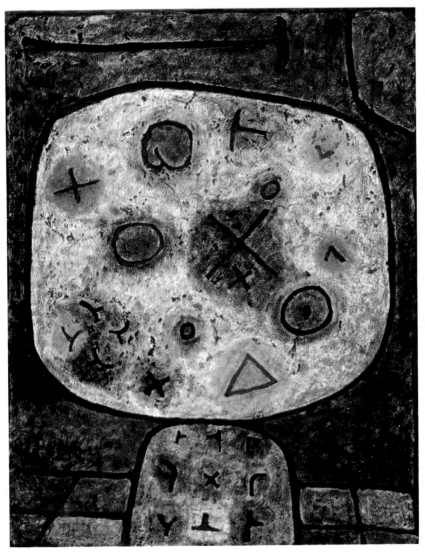

83 *Flower in a Stone.* 1939. Oil. 19⅝″×15¾″. Lausanne, Cantonal Fine Arts Museum. Some 1939 works depict angels and Satan, clearly showing Klee's preoccupation with death.

84 *Woodlouse in Enclosure.* 1940. Pastel. 12¼" × 16⅛". Bern, Klee Foundation. Compared with the graceful *Insula Dulcamara* (Plate 80), this is amazingly bold and deliberately crude.

85   *Woman in National Costume.*   1940. Gouache. 19″ × 12⅜″.   Bern, Klee Foundation.   The linear strength of Klee's symbolism is never more obvious than here.

86 *Tall Standing Aborigine.* 1940. Oil and charcoal. 27½″×19⅝″. Bern, Klee Foundation. **Klee's** fascination with Africa is well demonstrated in this grotesque work.

87 *Dark Journey*. 1940. 11⅝″ × 16¼″. Bern, Felix Klee Collection. Klee's fear of dying is shown in this horrible look into a world of demons and darkness.

88 *Double.* 1940. Color in paste medium. 20½″ × 13½″. Bern, Klee Foundation. His brave attempt to return to the simpler forms of a happy past.

89 *Drummer*. 1940. Gouache. 13¾″ × 8¾″. Bern, Klee Foundation. Late works like this anticipate
the bold draughtsmanship of Abstract Expressionism.

90   *Death and Fire*.   1940.   Oil 18⅛″×17⅜″.   Bern, Klee Foundation.   The grinning face of death, and strong hints of a mysterious African adventure.

91 *Still Life*. 1940. Oil. 39¼″×31½″. Bern, Felix Klee Collection. To the last, the mystical moon and the symbols of his new tongue.